Jack Wears Glasses ar JUST LIKE YOU!

Story by Juliette Vignola

Illustrated by Helen Dwiyanti

Author's Note

This is my third book in the "JUST LIKE YOU!" collection. My goal is to show our children with visual impairments that there are other children all over the world who share their struggles, and that glasses, contact lenses, patching and eye doctor visits are just a small part of life!

This book, "Jack Wears Glasses and a Patch... JUST LIKE YOU!" walks through a day in the life of Jack, a little boy who wears glasses and a patch. We see Jack playing with cars with his sister and going to the zoo, spending time at the eye doctor and sitting in the "Not so Scary" chair, and going for ice cream afterwards as a reward for good cooperation. Jack also gets eye drops from mommy and tries to cooperate, although he really does not like them!

See the last page of the book for useful tips from the author.

Other titles by Juliette Vignola:

Samantha Wears a Contact Lens and Patch... JUST LIKE YOU!
A day in the life of a unilaterally aphakic child

Jack Wears Contact Lenses and Glasses... JUST LIKE YOU!
A day in the life of a bilateral aphakic child

This is Jack!

**Jack likes to read books
and play with cars with his sister.**

Jacks wears glasses, JUST LIKE YOU!

When Jack wakes up in the morning, he cannot see very much at all until he puts on his glasses.

That's much better!

**Do you see the line across Jack's glasses?
That means that they are bifocal glasses.
Not all glasses are bifocal. Are yours?**

When Jack's glasses get dirty, he hands them to his mommy and she wipes them clean with a soft cloth. Jack hates wearing dirty glasses!

Sometimes Jack must wear a patch over one eye. This helps both of his eyes to be strong and to work together.

**Jack likes blue patches the best.
What color is your favorite?**

Jack is a good boy!
He doesn't take his patch off until
Mommy tells him it is the right time.

When Jack cooperates with his glasses and patch, he gets to choose a toy from the reward basket. Toy trains are his favorite!

Jack visits the eye doctor often to make sure that his eyes are healthy. He tries to stay very, very still while the doctor looks in his eyes.

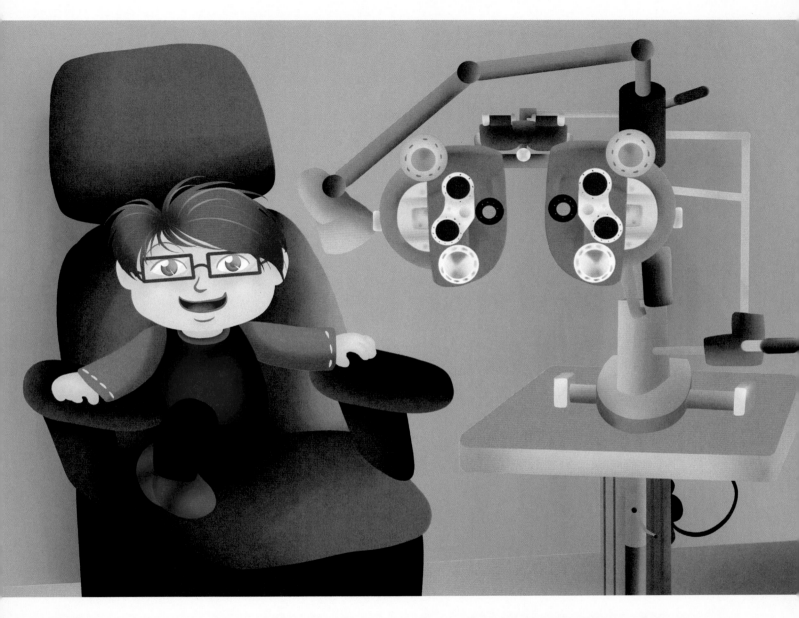

When Jack was little he was afraid of the doctor's chair. Now he calls it the "Not So Scary" chair. It is fun to look through the doctor's tools!

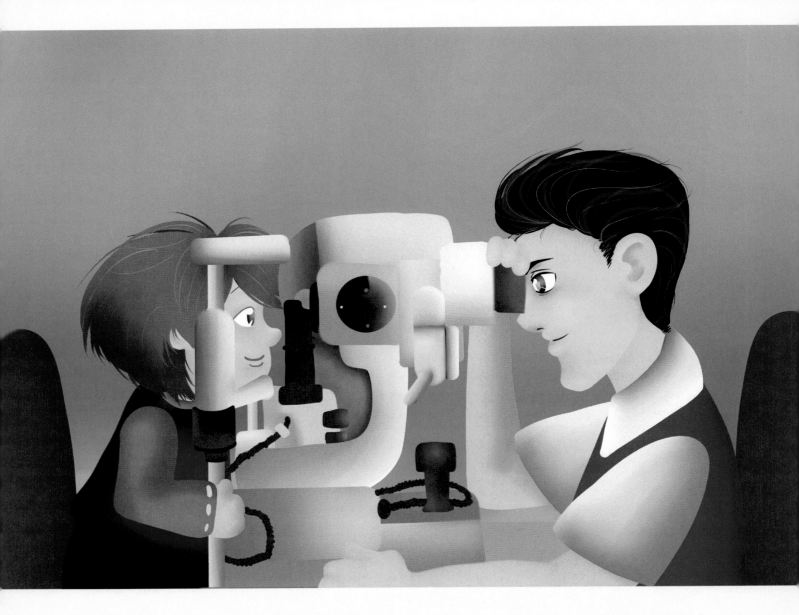

The doctor tells Jack to look straight ahead and pretend he is driving a space ship! Do you see the lights of the stars yet Jack? Keep looking!

Jack covers one eye and tells the doctor what letters he can see on the eye chart. Next he switches eyes and does it all over again!

Sometimes Jack's mommy has to put in eye drops. Jack calls them his Eye Tickles! Jack doesn't like the eye drops, but he tries his best to cooperate.

**When Jack cooperates at the eye doctor,
the whole family goes out for ice cream!
Everyone is happy when Jack cooperates!**

Jack even wears his glasses in the bathtub! Mommy has a dry cloth waiting for when the glasses get wet.

At bedtime, it is hard for Jack to see in the dark without his glasses. Jack has a night light to help him see where he is going.

**When Jack and his friends play outside,
they wear sunglasses and hats to keep
the sun out of their eyes.**

Jack's glasses and patch work together to help him to see more clearly.

Lots of children all over the world wear glasses and patches. It is important to take very good care of our eyes so that we can see all of the wonderful things around us!

More notes from the author...

Each child and parent is different, what worked for me may not work for you. But here are some tips you may find useful with your child.

1. If possible, get two pair of glasses. That way when your child resists wearing the glasses, they can choose which glasses to wear. They don't get to choose NOT to wear the glasses, but at least they have some control over what glasses to wear. Also, if one pair breaks or gets lost, you have a backup!

2. The key to patching is consistency. Many children go through a period where they rip off 10+ patches each day. Just stick with it! When they realize that they have to wear the patch, they often stop fighting patch time.

3. Reward charts can also be effective in helping to gain compliance with glasses and patching.

4. Books and web sites which feature photos of other kids in glasses can really go a long way toward helping your child to see that there are so many other children out there wearing glasses! There are also some really cool web sites for clothing for kids in glasses. Check out "Eye Power Kids Wear" and "Little Four Eyes", they are both AWESOME resources and web sites full of information!

5. You may also be interested in learning about vision therapy. Check out the Facebook pages "Vision therapy Parents Unite" and also "Vision Therapy Changed My Life". I have no personal experience with vision therapy but it sounds like something that holds promise for our children with developing eyesight.

Visit my blog at www.juliettevignola.com for more books for aphakic children and for other tips and tricks to deal with Aphakia and other vision issues!

Other Books in the "JUST LIKE YOU!" Collection
available on Amazon.com or www.juliettevignola.com

Jack Wears Contact Lenses and Glasses...
JUST LIKE YOU!
A day in the life of a bilateral aphakic child

Story by Juliette Vignola
Illustrated by Helen Dwiyanti

Samantha Wears a Contact Lens and Patch...
JUST LIKE YOU!
A day in the life of a unilateral aphakic child

Story by Juliette Vignola
Illustrated by Helen Dwiyanti

Made in the USA
Middletown, DE
30 January 2022